STAND

by

Tyari Witherspoon

authorHOUSE

1663 LIBERTY DRIVE, SUITE 200
BLOOMINGTON, INDIANA 47403
(800) 839-8640
www.authorhouse.com

First published by AuthorHouse 12/06/04

ISBN: 1-4184-1166-3 (sc)

Library of Congress Control Number: 2004105295

This book is printed on acid-free paper.

Printed in the United States of America
Bloomington, Indiana

Cover design by Tyari Witherspoon.

"Wherefore take unto you the whole armour of GOD, that ye may be able to withstand in the evil day, and having done all, to stand" (Ephesians 6:13).

TABLE OF CONTENTS

VOLUME ONE

What is Poetry? 2
I Want to Win Your Heart 3
Sweet Flower 5
I Apologize 6
Over You 8
Don't Settle For Less 10
Love and Respect 11
She's Your Lady 12
Single Mothers 13
Lost Children 15
Light and Liberation 16
Breath Spray 17
Born that Way 18
Stand 19
It Ain't About 21
Heaven for a G 22
Sell-Out 25
Here We Go Again 26
Black Caesar 29
We Have Arrived 31
Stars and Bars 35
My History 37
A Brother Gone Away 39
Maggie 40
Marshall 42
Blessed Eagle 43
Forgive and Forget 44
Keepin' It Real 45
Chain in the Rain 46
Jesus Is Listening 48
The Plight of Pure Hearts 49

VOLUME TWO

Mama 51
Little Man...53
What Is Love? 54
My Love is So Deep 55
Crazy 56
Rescue Me...57
Happily Ever After..58
You're Not Alone 59
Another Guy..60
The Truth About Macks 62
Watch the Doors..63
Cool Pity 64
I Got Yo' Nigga 65
No Doubt...66
Come Correct...68
Represent...70
All Hail the Black Queens 74
Black Is… 75
Equality...76
Black Oasis 77
Pecan Tan 78
For Stevie 79
Columbus Day 80
Racism...81
Glow..82
Ice Burns 83
Not the Way I Planned It..84
Flames...85
Pain 86
Puddles..87
21...88
Walk On 89
Water Under the Bridge 90
Wind or Wave...91
Mr. Stress 92
The End...93

Different Cymbal 94
In All My Ways 96
My Guide 97
Happy Birthday 98
For You 99
Real Easter 100
More Than Any Other 101

VOLUME THREE

My Fire 103
My 1 + 9 105
Body and Soul 106
On Hold 107
It Cannot Be Denied 109
No Place I'd Rather Be 111
All Alone 112
Fat Cats 113
Mr. Hologram Man 114
Mansion in the Projects 118
If Darkest Heart Remains 119
For All the Critics Who Falsely Accuse You 'Cause They Can't Stand or
Understand What They See In You 121
Metamorphosis 123
I Won't Let You Fall 124
Commentary 125
About the Author 137

To GOD Be The Glory!

First and foremost, I would like to thank GOD for enabling me to be blessed and to bless others through poetry. I would also like to thank everyone who has been of assistance or encouragement to me throughout the process of my writing and publications (probably, too many of you to name you all—but you know who you are and GOD bless)! I would also like to show much love to my family and friends, to all of our loved ones who have gone home to be with the Father, and to all those out there who know what it really means to keep it real. No doubt.

Dedication

This book is dedicated to my mother, a woman of GOD who knows and teaches others what it means to stand.

VOLUME ONE

What is Poetry?

Tell me,
what is poetry?
Poetry is love
and a gift from GOD above.
It is sun rays on a rose in bloom.
It drives away the dusk and gloom.
Tell me,
what is poetry?
Poetry is a crescent moon
or a junebug in June.
It's daisies and it's daffodils
or a late-night winter wind that chills.
It is many mountain snows
or retro like afros.
Tell me,
what is poetry?
Poetry is chocolate
and it's lollipops.
It's gospel, soul, and hip-hop.
It's hellos and goodbyes--
bright, blue skies and brown, teary eyes.
Sometimes contact to reject.
Sometimes abstract to reflect.
Tell me,
what is poetry?
It's all we hear,
touch, taste, smell, and see.
Poetry is you.
Poetry is me.

I Want to Win Your Heart

Close your eyes and count to ten.
When you are done you can open them again.
And you will find that I'm still standing there
with no intention of running anywhere
and hiding.

Facing what I'm feeling is hard to do.
But not as hard as losing you.

I want to win your heart.

Is it so hard to remember to call?
Have you been dodging me just like a ball?
How could you ever do me this way
when I would rather play house
with you some day?

If you're not ready, it is okay.
But can't we at least start talking today?

I want to win your heart.

I am too proud to beg--you will find.
But I'd be so proud, I'd brag if you were mine.
You do not have to be tagged to be "it."
When this world gets you down,
don't you ever forget
that to me you're special.

Knowing that my lost heart has been found,
I could never hurt you or let you down.

I want to win your heart.

Just like it's freeze…tag, I cannot move.

3

Only your warm embrace can soothe
or melt my lonely heart away.
So let us not play games another day.
Isn't it in your eyes, beautiful baby?
Say you will be my prize, lovely lady.

I want to win your heart.

Sweet Flower

Her soft voice speaks love--
that young lady as graceful as a dove
with jet-black hair streaming down with care
at such an uncommon length.
Such a pure heart and mind is so hard to find,
especially with such strength.
Beautiful is the hue in wondrous brown eyes true
and as bright as the sun.
Look for a sweeter flower than she,
and you will find none.

I Apologize

I never meant to let you down.
I only want to see you smile and never frown.
I never meant to cause you pain.
I hope you don't think that I
was just playing games
or just messing with your head.
I hope that you will understand
the truth instead.

One more chance is all I need
just to show you that you should be with me.
It's killing me to see the hurt still in your eyes.
I'll never hurt you again…
I apologize.

I guess that I was just afraid
because of the games that girls
in the past have played.
I should never have assumed you'd be the same.
Having not talked to you makes me so ashamed.
Never again will I be scared.
I'll make it up to you, girl,
and will always be there.

One more chance is all I need
just to show you that you should be with me.
It's killing me to see the hurt still in your eyes.
I'll never hurt you again…
I apologize.

Lady, understand me if you can.
Let me be your friend for now,
maybe later, your man.
I never ever should have let
bad things in the past get in the way

of what could finally be
a true love that could last always.

One more chance is all I need
just to show you that you should be with me.
It's killing me to see the hurt still in your eyes.
I'll never hurt you again…
I apologize.

Over You

You say I should give you one more chance,
but I must say that it is out of my hands.
My heart and mind have healed,
and each one says
I deserve better and should not settle for less.
You compared me to some of your friends,
and you even said that I did not fit in.
I was justified in getting so mad,
wondering how you could have treated me so bad.
How could you show me off
in front of friends and family,
but tell lies and play your games
when it was just you and me?
You knew for what I stood
and that I would be strong,
but that did not make it right
for you to treat me so wrong.

But it doesn't matter anymore.
No, not anymore.
Ever since the last time
that I walked out your door.
Now, did you really think I'd be waiting
with open arms for you?
I cannot and I will not.
I've gotten over you.

You say that I should give you one more chance,
but I must say that now it's out of my hands.
My heart and mind have healed,
and each one says
I deserve better and should not settle for less.
Who are you to try to tell me what ain't fair,
even if by some miracle I still cared?
When I needed you, you were never there.

But to convince me that you really care—
now you dare.
Toying with my emotions gave you pleasure,
and that's the reason why...I'm truly gone forever.

But it doesn't matter anymore.
No, not anymore.
Ever since the last time
that I walked out your door.
Did you really think I'd be waiting
with open arms for you?
I cannot and I will not.
I've gotten over you.

You spoiled and killed everything.
and as far as I can tell,
if our relationship is dead,
it should be buried, so farewell.
To change my mind,
there's nothing you can say or do.
You have to get over me, too.
I've gotten over you.

Don't Settle For Less

There are many more dogs than men in this world,
And it seems that they get most of the girls.
No matter how backwards that may seem,
That's how it is, and you know just what I mean.
Why would you ever be one man's trophy
When you could be another man's queen?
Ladies, maybe you think you can change a sorry man,
But you cannot really, and no one else can.
A man must change for himself—not for you,
He won't even change for his own child…
To trap yourself in misery is not meant for you to do.
If he abuses or disrespects you, he's no real man.
So find a man who is a man--one who will stand.
No matter how few in number they may seem to be,
Good men do exist and some are S-A-V-E-D.
A real man will be at your side, loyally.
He'll try to treat you nothing less than royally.
You don't have to put up with some guy's mess.
Wait for a real man to come, and until he does,
just be patient and don't settle for less.

Love and Respect

How can you call yourself loving somebody else
if you can't love yourself enough
to respect yourself enough
to only be with someone who will also respect you?

She's Your Lady

She's your lady,
and if she's your lady...
then you don't ever need a reason,
a special day, or holiday season
just to show how much you really love her
and that you are thinking of her.
Treat her well each day of your life.
Instead of shacking up forever,
make her your wife.
Don't expect her to cook and clean for you all the time--
even if wedding bells chime.
It's not about the things that you can buy.
She may still be up crying late at night.
It's the little things you do to share your time
that really make her feel real fine.
If the LORD really brought you together,
you will stand by your lady
in good or bad weather.
She is yours, and you are hers.
Each day, give her the care that she deserves.
Because she's your lady.
She's your lady.

Single Mothers

Now, watch what you say
'cause words can "kill"
in a sense, and its so hard to heal.
If you see an unmarried girl
about to bring a child into this world,
don't judge 'cause no matter the means--
if the child is born,
the birth must have been GOD's will.
He creates all life--it must have been His will.

I know that the Father
can bless all children and their mothers.
I know that the Father
takes care of faithful single mothers.

You may not know her circumstance.
Nothing in this world happens by chance.
For all you know,
the daddy could have run away.
Not every guy that makes a baby
is man enough to stay.
Some are out populating the world
all on their own,
and increasing the burdens of the women
they've left alone.
But a lady does not need a man to stand
forever and always.
Gets lonely--but with faith in GOD,
it won't always be this way.
The right man, He'll send along some day.

I know that the Father
can bless all children and their mothers.
I know that the Father
takes care of faithful single mothers.

13

Do women of divorce and separation
deserve the attacks on their reputations?
The verse "what GOD has put together,
let no man put asunder"
gets run in the ground
and needs to be buried six feet under
when it is taken out of context.
Don't you know that common sense
should tell you that women don't have to stay
with psychologically, physically, or otherwise abusive men.
Most marriages are not put together by GOD
in the first place.
Instead people rush into marriage,
and it ends up being a waste in the worst case.

I know that the Father
can bless all children and their mothers.
I know that the Father
takes care of faithful single mothers.

Take a look at the people you have known in your days.
Some of the children of single mothers were the best raised.

Lost Children

How could you throw away your children?
How could you cast your child away
when somebody somewhere is wishing
they had a little one to raise?
How could you deprive them of their chance
to live, to laugh, and to learn every day as they grow?
Life begins at conception,
even if it doesn't show.

How could you say the children you have
are nothing?
Why won't you teach them a better way?
How could you say
they won't amount to anything
when already they have the potential
to make it some day?

Light and Liberation

Light is to the sun
as liberation is to education.

Breath Spray

I prefer breath mints—they're okay.
But I've got no love for breath sprays.
Unless it happens to be all natural,
you're blasting your mouth with something flammable.
You're better off being a hot breath blower
than carrying a mini flame thrower.
Peppermint or cinnamon.
How do you like your carcinogen?

Born that Way

Because every human has male and female tendencies,
one's sex is determined by one's anatomy.
Don't mistake such tendencies for a call to homosexuality.
Sexuality, as well as other roles, is learned through socialization,
Nobody is born homosexual.
It is a choice that some humans make.
Humans have the ability to reason.
Sometimes it is faulty reasoning.
Animals rely basically on instinct.
When have you ever seen gay animals?

Stand

Don't pop tops and don't bust caps.
Brothers, be too strong for that.
You don't have to slang to live phat.
You don't deserve your props
if you're down with that--
down with the wack--
down with the negative stereotypes
of positive Black.
It is better to be strong than to be hard,
and it is better to be assertive than to be aggressive.
While strength and stability are respectable,
a hot head and a bad attitude are not at all impressive.
Frontin' hard and acting tough does not make you a man.
Only standing for what's right can.
The mark of a man is the ability to stand.
Even when you must stand alone.
Sometimes, you have to stand alone.
Control your own mind.
Don't follow the crowd.
To excel in school is cool.
You're still Black, so be proud.
Set the right examples
for little brothers growing up.
It will encourage them when they see in you
a strong Black man showing up.
And when you're on or off the scene,
always treat your woman like a precious,
beautiful, Black queen.
Above all, you need JESUS.
Accept Him as your Lord
and personal savior, today.
Walk with Him and talk with Him.
Put your hand in His hand to stay.
In times good or bad, repent and always pray.
If you live right, He will empower you to stand.

19

If you don't, you'll go to hell,
and that ain't cool, man.
Would you rather have heaven or hell?
Would you rather chill or burn?
Would you rather die or learn?
Real change comes slow,
but change will come, though.
If you're afraid to run to it,
you can walk or at least crawl.
Black men should be strength's epitome
instead of hand puppets for the enemy.
Make the choice to stand.
You don't have to fall.

It Ain't About ...

It ain't about
what society tells us is being a man.
It ain't about
being hard.
Hard and strong are two different things.
It ain't about
cussin' every other word that comes out your mouth.
It ain't about
how much you can drink
without falling over.
It ain't about
how much weed you can smoke.
It ain't about
lying and cheating.
It ain't about
gettin' yours
and forgettin' your woman and children.
It ain't about
dominating women.
It ain't about
how many women you can get.
It ain't about
how much hell you can raise.
Heaven should be your goal in all your days.

Heaven for a G

Let me holler at all of my peeps in the street.
We've been deceived.
There ain't no heaven for a G.
The devil wants to trick us
'til we take our last breath.
Then it's too late and we got no time left
for our souls to be saved.

The devil comes to steal, kill, and destroy.
He wants to corrupt our girls and boys.
He comes as a roaring lion
seeking whom he may devour.
That's why kids are killing kids
on the news hour.
The devil wants our souls.
So he fills our heads with visions of gold,
fancy clothes, fancy cars, money to burn,
and a mentality that says we don't have to earn...
Some rich, racist, greedy whites—
they don't want to live with you.
But if they want their drugs sold,
they know who to give it to.
They think it's better us than them
when it comes to getting killed or busted.
Why do we let them use us like some puppets?

Let me holler at all of my peeps in the street.
We've been deceived.
There ain't no heaven for a G.
The devil wants to trick us
'til we take our last breath.
Then it's too late and we got no time left
for our souls to be saved.

We look up to the wrong people—

the ones who live illegal,
the ones caught up in all kinds dirt and evil.
Even if they had mad game,
we don't remember lost brothers
unless they also had fame.
Why do we reject GOD's truest believers
when GOD is the only one in this world
who will never leave us.
But we must repent.
He won't force Himself on us.
If we don't repent,
senseless tragedies will continue to fall upon us.
It takes a real man to stand,
but you can't be a real man without your hand
in GOD's hand.

Let me holler at all of my peeps in the street.
We've been deceived.
There ain't no heaven for a G.
The devil wants to trick us
'til we take our last breath.
Then it's too late and we got no time left
for our souls to be saved.

We know that dogs just want to have their way and dash.
So why we disrespecting our bodies for the cash?
Have we forgot about STDs and HIV?
Cheap sex, alcohol, and drugs first kill us
spiritually and mentally,
and then physically, eventually.
Every day, we selling our souls.
We poppin' caps now—
ain't no more pourin' coals.
Don't we know that we punks if we can't fight
without a gun or a knife?
How can we take another brother's life?
Real gangs run the organized crime.

23

We just some wannabees out here on the streets dying.
Manipulated and so blind that we don't care
or just don't understand.
If we've been programmed to hate ourselves,
we can't help but hate the brother man.
But it's time for Blacks killing Blacks
to become played out.
It's time to stand for what's right
instead of always taking the easy way out.
It's time for love
and solidarity.
It's time for victory
through a closer walk with GOD,
which starts with clarity.

Let me holler at all of my peeps in the street.
We've been deceived.
There ain't no heaven for a G.
The devil wants to trick us
'til we take our last breath.
Then it's too late and we got no time left
for our souls to be saved.

The enemy wants us to be destroyed. True.
But let's take some accountability for ourselves.
Stand up and be strong Black men and women
no matter the cost.
With this generation, let's make a change.
Too many souls have already been lost.

Sell-Out

Are you a sell-out
or just a fool?
Why be the slave of foreign drug lords
and the rich whites who let illegal drugs come here?
That ain't cool!
They think of each of you as clowns!
You make them richer while helping to keep your own people down!
Even if I felt I had to,
I could not resort to a life of crime.
There is no crime that could only endanger me.
Do I have the right to destroy somebody's family
or help to make a crack baby?

Here We Go Again

Here we go again.
What goes around comes back around again.
Here we go again.
Be it your enemy, your family, or your friend.

Each and every day as we live,
treat others like you want to be treated,
and if they don't, then you forgive.
When an evil act is done, does it ever end
when we ain't got enough sense to kneel and repent?
So full of ill will and ill intent,
living so foul that we have a foul scent.
Look at the time we have spent
on destruction bent.
Trifling and ignorant, but playing innocent.
So full of anger and hate that we become begrudged.
Won't budge, but ready to explode at the slightest nudge.
Lord forbid that we take it to our dying bed
like some have done and carried grudges
'til they were dead.
I know it hurts,
but you gotta let it go.
Give it to GOD.
Act like you know.

I'm not trying to put you down or to offend you.
But if you don't break the cycle,
it will continue…

Here we go again.
We're so quick to say that nobody can fade us.
Here we go again.
But fail to realize how kids imitate us.

I once was lost, but now I'm found.

I'm making leaps, I'm making bounds.
When I come around,
give me props and give me pounds
'cause I put it down
and I can never be clowned.
This is how it sounds
when my voice resounds
resonant and clear.
Ya feel me up in here?
Ya ever shed a tear
for your peers
because they chose the wrong path
and found hell's aftermath?
We dirty and we need a bath—
go ahead and laugh.
But it's serious business.
Can I get a witness?
If you're fed up, had enough, put your hands up.
When are the real men gonna stand up
and set the proper examples for our kids
and teach them to do better than what we did?
I'm sick of it—
not sick wit' it—
The way we run from responsibility
in futility instead of learning humility.
We can't just blame somebody else all the time.
It's time for self-accountability.

I'm not trying to put you down or to offend you.
But if you don't break the cycle,
it will continue…

Here we go again.
Thought about it again and again in your mind,
and no, it ain't cool.
Here we go again.
So tell me,

how many times you gonna play the fool?

Why are you literally or figuratively,
like retail, selling your body?
Your peace and your self-respect
are more important than material things.
Don't trade your dignity for the "make-up gifts"
that some lying, cheating brother brings.
I can't handle this with kid gloves.
Not when I know it's time for tough love.
What is going on my sistas?
Why do you keep letting trifling brothers
get witcha?
You deserve mutual respect—
not all kinds of abuse and neglect.
A beat down is not a show of love and affection.
And no, he can't make up for it later
with an erec----.
Where is your mind—Venus or Saturn?
For your kids you sew a heckuva pattern.
Your children are more important
than some buster
not interested in commitment—only in play.
If you're not careful, some day
your little daughters will follow
the path that you lay.
If you don't teach them and lead by example
to resist whorish brothers,
they may become like you were—
a teenage mother.

Now, I'm not trying to put you down
or to offend you.
But if you don't break the cycle,
it will continue…

Black Caesar

Black Caesar, 1999
October 4, they blew my mind.
Somebody done turned my day
into a Shakespearean play.
Sneak attacked like Julius Caesar,
I had my conspirators
without being warned.
I been 'buked and I been scorned.
I found myself pulling sharp objects
from out of my back.
What up wit' dat?
Must be "open season" on Blacks.
I've heard about a knife in the back,
but these cats had straight up swords.
Satan sews discord,
but vengeance is mine—I will repay,
thus saith the LORD.
Some white folk think they got power
and that they can't be touched.
No, I don't hate them,
but I can say this much:
Any attack on me
is a challenge to my Father Almighty.
HE said "touch not my anointed
and do my prophet no harm"—
"the least of all you do unto these my little ones,
you do it unto me."
Now, who is big and bad enough
To stand against G-O-D?
No weapon formed against me shall prosper.
That's the truth—that's the straight up gospel.
I can tell any man, woman, boy, or girl:
Greater is He that is in me
than he that is in the world.
You can plot against GOD's anointed

all day and all night.
But that which is done in the dark
shall be brought to light.
If you dig a ditch for me, go ahead and dig two—
I suggest.
'Cause you next.
I will rise above it all and still confess
that I am better than blessed.

We Have Arrived

Don't ignore problems just because you find them distasteful.
When you do, you just recycle them
and it's just wasteful.
Too many of our young roses never bloom.
It's fear and gloom
because they've been consumed
by abuse, "offers they cannot refuse,"
drug abuse, and sex predators on the loose.
Hurt and confused,
some rise above it, but others tie their own noose.

Not every brother can be an athlete or a rapper.
Even if he's Phi Beta Kappa
and magna cum laude like me, he's gonna see
he's not invited to the party.
If his skin's some shade of brown or sounds Black on paper
it can be rough going up on the elevator—
especially if you started in the basement...
Society's materialism smells so sweet that you can taste it.
So then you're tempted with crime on the lo-lo,
risking your life and running from the po-po.
What a disgrace when we embrace
that which has robbed our own race.

This goes out to my minorities,
who are poor, frustrated, and lacking opportunities.
We get tracked, and it ain't cool
the way we get pushed through school.
Institutionalized racism sets us up to fail.
We're pushed out because
they would rather see us in jail.
Through this type of adversity,
they try to discourage us
from attending universities.
Many rich whites oppose

leveling the playing field
and refuse to yield.
They don't care about
how disadvantaged you may be.
A privileged class
does not give up its privilege willingly.
I never understood
why just because they live in richer neighborhoods
that they should get a better education.
And they expect us to believe that all are equal
in this nation.
The few rich Blacks we have are not considered upper class
because their money is first generation.
Racist cops pull us over in our fancy cars
despite the fact that we're lawyers
by occupation.

Ask about discrimination
when you come around,
and we'll insist it don't exist—
no, not in our town.
I knew a chief named Webb
who had to experience the flow of an ebb.
They put him through some hell
just because he did his job too well.
He was a righteous man,
and that should have been his evidence.
Still he lost his job because of white prejudice.
They might have won some battles,
but my GOD will win the war.
I ain't forgot about the VA and Moore's.
Just the good old boys,
but they mean us some harm.
Racists claiming to love GOD
are gonna keep the devil warm.

Since many whites have been the friend of me,

I would be the first to say that most whites
are not my enemy.
Unfortunately, it does not take a large number—
as far as I've been seeing.
It only takes a few to try to maintain a system
that existed before this country
even came into being.

We didn't have a "drug problem"
as long as it was Black kids.
We didn't have a "gun control" problem
until there were more and more White kids.
They can't deny it when I tell them
that Blacks don't ship drugs and guns.
They just give them to us to sell them.

Right now we're in a knock down, drag down
trying to pull the white racist flag down.
In this country, we have state and federal government.
So, on top of our capitol buildings,
the confederate flag does not belong.
We are right and not wrong.
Our conviction is so strong.
This has gone on too long.

How can some of us get rich,
forget where we came from,
and sell out completely?
It's ludicrous and just plain dumb
to say we don't need things
like affirmative action and EEOC.*
It's 2000, but still every now and then
we experience "whites only" all over again.
Some of us still get shot or beaten so vicious.
They say we look suspicious.
We all look alike…
Yeah, right!

For too long we've been deprived.
To reach new heights we must continually strive
each and every day of our lives
if we're gonna survive.
Oh, we got it made.
We have arrived.

Please see the 'Commentary' section.

Stars and Bars

They would want the confederate flag taken down as much as we do
if descendants of poor whites would recognize the truth.
Then they would hate the flag,
want to deface the flag,
erase the flag, never embrace the flag.
Instead of being birds of a feather,
it was rich whites who invented the
term "poor white trash"—
so put 2 and 2 together.
They manipulated poor Whites against Blacks and minorities
in order to maintain their social position
and retain their authority.
How does it feel to be used
and as a result, to be confused?
Plain and simply stated,
hate destroys the hater, not the hated.
Hate groups are trying to recruit
a new generation,
leading them to the path of eternal damnation.
A burned down church and broken glass—
would they have hated Christ
for having skin of burnt brass?**
This country would have met an early grave
if not for the strong back of a slave!
Yet, he never got his 40 acres and a mule.
For his contributions, no recognition,
not even minuscule.
For another year, we have to celebrate
the birth of Dr. King
with the pain that the waving of the stars and bars brings.
If the American flag truly defines us,
why does our government allow
the Confederate flag to remind us
of enslavement, rape of our women, whippings, separation of our families,
lynchings, and all that which devastates?

35

The confederate flag has always been
and still is a symbol of hate,
white supremacy, and this nation's division.
Our endeavor to remove it permanently
from our state capitol building and grounds
is a holy and righteous mission.

**Please see the 'Commentary' section.

My History

What was once the world's most powerful
and richest region
is now a poverty, famine-stricken legion.
Ric Flair says, "to be the man,
you have to beat the man."
But in order to keep him down,
claiming credit for his great contributions,
creating the myth of his inferiority, and destroying as much as possible
of his written history are the solutions.
This is why we know even less
about our ancestry
despite the fact that some African oral history
says there was African civilization
around 25,000 B.C.

Why have they tried to take away my history?
Why have they tried to take away my legacy?
They had to erase my identity
in order to promote white supremacy.

How come our children are not taught
that Africa is the mother of civilization?
Ancient "Ethiopia" was the mother of Kham or Kemet,
the so-called Egypt,
and is older than any other known "nation."
Although it was Europe who was illiterate
during the "Dark Ages,"
it is the achievements of Africa's children
that are absent from history book pages.
Our scholarship is met with adversity
despite the fact that Africans gave Europe its first universities.
In Africa, before the white man came,
there already existed Christianity.
Still, some Europeans had the nerve
to use Christianity

to justify slavery.
Why aren't students taught that Africa
and its colored children
were teachers of the world, not just the pupils?
Why do white favoring school systems still exist—
systems without scruples?
Why did there have to be suffering
(to gain us the civil rights
that all people should be born with)
by our earlier generations?
Nothing that took centuries to build
disappears "overnight."
Why does institutionalized racism still exist
in this "all that" nation?
Why are we still uninformed and misinformed?
Let me guess.
If accurate information contradicts white supremacy,
it gets suppressed.

Why have they tried to take away my history?
Why have they tried to take away my legacy?
They had to erase my identity
in order to promote white supremacy.

A Brother Gone Away
(For Rock)

After two months of sharing a dorm room,
the brother's gone away.
It was even stranger having seen him in a dream
just before his dying day.
At first, it was hard to believe
that it was even real,
even if it was less emotional than psychological what I would feel.
Of some things going on in your mind
you are unaware
even when of death you are not scared.
What was our room
became my half empty room,
but the presence of GOD
protected against gloom.
We never became the best of buddies,
but for weeks afterwards,
it was difficult to do my studies.
Still, I overcame in Jesus' name.
You come to miss a new familiar face.
A familiar "stranger" gone,
but not without a trace.
The impermanence of human life is so clear.
At least three others around me are gone,
but GOD has kept me here.
I thank GOD that my new semester
will be my new start,
while with his loved ones is my heart.
I pray that we will always remember
that with faith in GOD,
even when we do not understand,
we remain forever in His hands.

Maggie

A sweet branch in the family tree,
did you know what you meant to
my family and me?
Anytime, if no one else, we could depend on
Al and Maggie Lee.
Everyone can think of times past
when you would have given
even if it was your last.
We all have one life to live.
Only GOD has life to give.
Why do we question when He decides to take it?
Before you left us for heaven,
you knew you would make it.
It is not the taking of a life, anyway.
Because for the deceased,
it's the beginning of a new day.
I know you're up in heaven looking down.
I done finally came up,
and I know that you're proud.
Thank you for the encouragement and support
in some of my most frustrating days
in college and in Columbia
trying to find a job that pays.
You were so different and we miss you so much.
I thank GOD for all the lives that through you,
He has touched.
Overwhelmed, right now I think of you.
I wish that more could be said than just
"I love you."

I'm always gonna love ya,
dear aunt, dear friend, second mother.
I'm always gonna love ya
dear aunt, dear friend, second mother.

Always so protective, you always prayed.
Praise the LORD that I am saved--
I know that way
I'm gonna see you again someday.
I thank GOD for showing me your smile
in a dream.
Everything will be all right
'cause we on GOD's team.
And that's with no ifs, no buts, and no maybes.
Like my little cousin that you kept used to say,
"I love you, baby."

I'm always gonna love ya,
dear aunt, dear friend, second mother.
I'm always gonna love ya,
dear aunt, dear friend, second mother.

You now reside in a place
with no pain and no pressure,
experiencing joy beyond measure.
With Carlos and Uncle Al,
it's "one love" we feel.
And always, you know we still real.

I'm always gonna love ya,
dear aunt, dear friend, second mother.

Marshall

I'm paying my respects to real heroes unsung.
Sometimes, the good die young.
Who knows if death will be the way we overcome?
GOD is the only one.

I thank the LORD for letting me live
to see another day.
Once again, I find myself writing about a brother gone away.
But this time its family, spiritual family.
A man of GOD to look up to
is what you've been to me.
You were a good son to your father,
to all a good brother and a good friend.
To your children a good father,
to your wife a good husband.
Saved, sanctified, and Spirit-filled
prayer warrior, you always stayed real.
It felt bad to hear to that you're gone,
but it feels good to know that you're home.

I'm paying my respects to real heroes unsung.
Sometimes, the good die young.
Who knows if death will be the way we overcome?
GOD is the only one.

If anyone wonders
why the LORD would take such a young man,
let us remember that GOD is all-wise,
and we as humans will not always understand.
You were a bold preacher of the gospel
just like your father.
Your life was written so well by the world's greatest Author.
There's consolation in knowing it is not the end,
but the beginning of a new story.
The angels in heaven rejoice,
and GOD has for you a home in His glory.

Blessed Eagle

One night he took to the sky
only to be shot down.
It was hard to get back up and try again
to leave the ground.
But this eagle is strong,
though his shrieks are not always loud.
His wingspan is wide and long.
There is pride in his glide--so proud.
He is brown but Black with soul song.
He won't retreat--
not even at the sight
of rain clouds.
For he knows the rain must soon pass,
and he knows he must survive every storm.
Bright is his vision,
though dark are his eyes of glass.
The world around him is so cold,
but his heart remains warm.
Sometimes he must soar far away,
but he always returns to the same nest.
Free to float out of your sight,
he knows that he is blessed.

Forgive and Forget

You've forgiven,
but you haven't forgotten
'cause you're not sure that it's humanly possible.
Memories of your past are often so very vivid,
yet your faith in GOD
has made you indomitable.
But you should know GOD won't let you forget all of the bad things
He freed you from, and He is great.
If you forgot everything,
it would be awfully hard
to remember where you came from
and to appreciate
where you are now, and still you will overcome.
Though the words "forgive and forget"
are much more easily said than done.
What does that phrase really mean anyway?
Will you wake up tomorrow with no recollection of events of yesterday?
"I'm sorry" should be accepted,
but it doesn't always fix things as far as I've seen.
That we should forgive and not hold grudges
is what "forgive and forget"
was intended to mean.

Keepin' It Real

Keepin' it real--
For real.
Sometimes
Keepin' it real
Really hurts.
Sometimes
A heart of gold
Gets thrown away
For a clump of dirt!
Dissed
Due to your strength.
Feared
For your maturity.
Misunderstood
In your spirituality.
Exposed to
(But freed from)
obscurity!
Walking
Under a power
Ignored.
Not exalting yourself--
Just the Lord.
Your elders see--
Like you.
Children respect--
Want to be like you.
For real.
That's on the real.
Know to whom
You belong.
Keep your head up.
Keep strong.
Keep on
Keepin' it real.

45

Chain in the Rain

My dear LORD,
please don't let me be here alone.
Although I have done some wrong,
help me to stay strong.
I've felt so much pain.
When are things going to change?
When will I break the chain
in the rain?

I don't understand.
When there's not a single cloud in view,
and the skies seem so bright blue,
how does the rain still come falling through?
Why is there still anger and frustration
when reminded of old mess
even though I know I am truly blessed.
Free me from all this I'm feeling.
I need Your help.
I need Your healing.

LORD, oh, LORD,
please don't let me be here all alone.
Although I have done some wrong,
help me to stay strong.
I've felt so much pain.
When are things going to change?
When will I break the chains
outside in the rain?

Soon, it all is going to pass.
Nothing so sad can ever last.
So in it, I will not be consumed.
Peace and victory are coming soon.
My sweet Lord
will not let me be alone.

Although I have done some wrong,
He will keep me strong.
Things will soon change.
Freedom from pain I'll surely gain,
and I will break the chain
in the rain.

Jesus Is Listening

Jesus is listening to all I say.
He supplies all my needs because in faith I pray.
He is a lawyer who has no fee
and a doctor with medicine
guaranteed to heal me.
I never have to doubt
that He will be there on time.
True friends are few in number,
but it's so good to know
that Jesus is always mine.
GOD always hears
and frees my fears.
His Spirit is near,
and so life is never as bad as it appears.
Even if tomorrow
seems not a sunny day
because of trouble or sorrow,
Jesus is still mine,
and He hears me when I pray.

The Plight of Pure Hearts

Why are the people with the biggest hearts
often the hearts who get stepped on
over and over again
as if it doesn't mean a thing?
Why are the ones who are phony
and up to no good never lonely
while the purest hearts
often feel a knife's sting?

I can tell you why.
When light comes, darkness flies.
Just hold on, I'd advise.
GOD always hears our cries.

Why are the people with the biggest hearts
often the ones who get let down
time and time again
as if it won't matter at all?
Why are the ones full of deception
leading people in the wrong direction
while those who really care
are there for them when they call?

I can tell you why.
When light comes, darkness flies.
Just hold on, I'd advise.
GOD always hears our cries.

Why are the people with the biggest hearts
often the ones who are put down
by and by and by
and they feel they have few friends?
Why are the ones who are God-less,
so cold-hearted, and thoughtless?
They prosper now, but those who suffer
for righteousness will in the end.

VOLUME TWO

Mama

I love you, dear mother.
You raised us well.
You held us up
and never let us down.
And like no other,
you deeply care,
and you are always there
when no one else can be found.
For us, you prayed both night and day.
From day to day,
you showed us how to love our Lord and ourselves.
Far back as I can remember,
you took care of us
when we could not take care of ourselves.
Corrected us when we did wrong.
Gentle when possible.
But when needed, firm and strong.
You've always known when we were hurt.
Motherly instinct to hold us and to provide comfort.
You wiped our eyes
when we would cry.
And still support us as adults
in our most trying of times.
A lovely smile on a beautiful face
a caring word, a mother's kiss,
and a warm embrace.
Your faith and love
cannot be replaced.
No matter what goes wrong, your strength,
this world cannot erase.
You have shown us how to stand,
put all our trust in GOD,
and never live cowardly.
To still treat others respectfully
even when they do not deserve it

and treat us hurtfully.

Mama,
You've been my friend.
Teacher,
You've been my guide.
Pastor,
You've shown me how to live a saved life.
Mama,
You've taught me to live in love and not die in pride.

I can never repay you
for all you've done,
but thank you
for letting your light so shine.
I love you, dear mother.
You sacrificed
in your life
and made the difference in mine.

Little Man

From my name yours was derived.
How you have touched all of our lives.
The unconditional love of a child
that can make me forget my troubles with your smile.
You balled up your fists
and held your own bottle at the age of 5 days.
You did a "one-hander" at 2 weeks,
and at 8 months, said "hallelujah" for GOD's praise.
It's unbelievable—
the speed with which you crawl across the floor.
Heartwarming when you rush to me
as I enter Grandma's door.
It is you that your mother
and we all adore.
You walk—even run
as long as we're holding both your hands.
But soon you will walk on your own.
You can always look up to me, "little man."
You will never be alone.

What Is Love?

What is love?
Is it GOD above…
or is it selfishness
and personal gain?
Is love pleasure?
Is love pain?
Is it responsibility?
Is it trust?
Is it a bond,
or is it just lust?
Is love sex?
Is it manipulation?
Is it a game
meant for "spectation"?
Can we deposit or withdraw love
like a bank transaction?
Is love just a feeling…
or an action?

My Love is So Deep

Just as sure as the sky is light blue in the day
and deep purple to jet black in the night,
my love lives longer than the stars
and shines twice as bright.
As wide as the expanse of sky—
Deeper than Earth's core and the universe
which GOD created.
Only the love of GOD is greater,
and neither can be faded.
Now that's deep…
But I can go deeper.

Crazy

You are a star from the sky
whose brightness can never die
and whose beauty catches my eye
when I see you passing by.
I'm going out of my mind
just trying to find
a way to tell you how I feel.
I'm for real.

I'm crazy…
It's true.
I'm crazy, and I cannot help it.
Crazy about you.
I'm crazy for you.
I wish that you were mine.

You are a star from above.
I have to try to win your love
and give to you the new book of my heart
that no one can tear apart.
I'll be a clown just to make you smile
or to laugh for a while.
I'll be your teddy bear
when you are hurt or scared.
If you give me a chance,
you'll see I've always cared.
I've always cared.

I'm crazy…
It's true.
I'm crazy, and I cannot help it.
Crazy about you.
I'm crazy for you.
I wish that you were mine.

Rescue Me

When your heart is broken,
it feels like you've been scarred,
and like your heart has been torn apart.
Time goes on and you get over this,
but it don't take away the loneliness
of your heart.
You need a brand new start.
You are more beautiful than any work of art.

Rescue me.
Rescue me from this lonely world I'm in.
Into your heart, let me in.
Never let me go back again.

Wish I may, wish I might
see you tonight.
You are like a finely crafted doll—
except you are real
and I can feel
the warmth of your eyes,
and how I love your smile.
GOD made you such a pretty child.
You're the lady whom I adore,
and I wish that I could see you more.
Your sweet love can bring me in from the storm
if your heart will open up the door.

Rescue me.
Rescue me from this lonely world I'm in.
Into your heart, let me in.
Never let me go back again.

Happily Ever After

I have you, and it's just like a dream come true.
Without you, what in the world would I do?
You've got me too.
And that is why you're never alone.
You don't have to face this cold world
on your own.

I love you so dearly.
I need to hold you near me.
I'll replace your tears with laughter,
and we'll live happily ever after.

With faith in GOD, all things are possible.
His love is so incredible.
So, let's create our triangle of love
with the two of us and with GOD above.
And this way, what we have will last forever.
Even beyond this world, we'll be together.

I love you so dearly.
I need to hold you near me.
I'll replace your tears with laughter,
and we'll live happily ever after.

You're Not Alone

There used to be a tendency
for me to let the past
mess up the chances I received.
Nothing could ever last.
But the past is gone, now I have healed,
and I know what to do.
You are my present,
and my future is with you.

You are not alone.
If no one else in all the world,
you will have me from now on.
You're not alone.

It seems so strange, so much has changed
since we have been together.
It feels so good to know you're real,
and baby, I will never
disrespect you, let you down,
or tear what we have apart.
Forever, you will be in my heart.

You are not alone.
If no one else in all the world,
you will have me from now on.
You're not alone.

Another Guy

I'm not just another guy.
I am called a man--
Not because I'm old,
but because I stand.
Why are some females so blind
that they do not recognize
how a good man goes out of his way
to bring them joy inside.

A man who really cares will always be around--
there to lift you up, even if he is down.

Guys are not the same.
They will bring you pain,
and deceive your vulnerable heart
right from the very start.
They'll often disrespect you
and will even neglect you.
But if you just open your eyes,
you'll see much brighter skies.

A real man will always stand right by your side.
When you hurt, he will wipe the tears
from your eyes.

A good woman deserves
someone who is only hers--
hers exclusively,
who'll never treat her abusively--
verbally, mentally, or physically.
Someone who'll never put her down,
but will always try to support her,
and always treat her like a lady.

Someone who'll never lay a hand

upon his only queen.
No woman should ever
settle for lesser things.

The Truth About Macks

You might have a nice body,
but that doesn't mean I'm out to get it.
I'm trying to be your friend,
not just trying to hit it.
If that's all you want,
you ought to be ashamed.
You better recognize.
That's not my game.
Game is for macks,
and macks are just dogs.
They "ho-hop" around like frogs.
You better wake up and resist
because a double-standard exists.
If a woman gets with more than one man,
people call her a "ho".
Now that's wack.
But when a man gets with more than one woman,
society says he's cool--
he's "just" a player or a mack.

Watch the Doors

Let us open wide the doors of our minds,
but let us not allow the enemy to come in
and build a wall where the doors once stood.

Cool Pity

Just as long as you are standing for what's right,
don't worry about their jeers.
It's alright to be mature beyond your years.
Who you are is not defined by your peers.
You are not better, but you can be stronger,
and with GOD on your side, you will last longer.
I would love for everywhere I go
to have a lot of peeps who are down—
straight props and straight pounds.
But I know that ain't reality.
Reality is being accepted by some
but dissed by so many.
But at least, those who have not seen yet
will see eventually.
Be a young, strong Black man on a mission,
with the courage and the vision
to make the right, yet unpopular decision.
To follow and please the crowd is a "cool pity".
My brother, be a man, and show some integrity.

I Got Yo' Nigga

I am not yo' nigger.
Tell me how you figure
that descendants of Black kings and queens
should accept a word intended to demean
our sisters and our brothers.
"Nigger-bit--" is what slave traders called
our enslaved African mothers.
Therefore, it is just plain absurd—
the way some of us today accept and use both of those words.
How can we build a strong Black nation
in the midst of the direct and indirect glorification
of the disrespect toward our women, drug abuse, violence, and sexual
promiscuity?
We need to take these things from perpetuity
into discontinuity.

Tyari Witherspoon

No Doubt

If you're like me,
and you miss hearing substance in rap,
let's shun all that commercialized crap!
"Anything for the papers" is their mentality.
"Anything for the papers"—bump originality.
Caught up in commercialism.
When I offer these criticisms,
they cannot deny them.
So, why do we try to justify them?
I talk about reality, too.
But I attack our problems—
they just glorify them.
All across the nation,
we want instant gratification—
even at the risk of eternal damnation.
It's ill-gotten gain—
temporary blessings from the devil.
As the foul money piles up,
down goes the spiritual level.
Some who claim to be positive
are not as positive as they claim.
Excessive profanity in 'socially conscious' songs
is like using gasoline to put out flames.
I'm looking and laughing at some of these cats
who claim they keep it real,
but really can't rap.
They got in the game by who they know
and because they're willing to make
these little minstrel shows—
calling brothers 'nigga' and calling women
"bit--es" and "hoes."
Selling meaningless sex
and thug life in our communities
and the belief that it's okay to get high.
Can we get real lyrical skills in the form of a drug to boost our immunity

systems?—Like 4th and goal, let's blitz them—
it's do or die.
People who uplift us should be our real heroes.
The music industry just wants to increase the number of zeros
behind the first digit
by selling negative stereotypes of our people. ***
I ain't wit' it.

I'm keepin' it real 'cause 'real' is the word.
I came to put it down,
ya heard?
I'm keepin' it real 'cause 'real' is the word.
I came to represent,
ya heard?

No doubt. No doubt.
This is what I rhyme about.

My illest flow to a beat that swings,
teaching kids that there's more to life than
bling-bling,
seeing our youth graduate like class rings—
these are a few of my favorite things—
like teaching girls to become queens
and boys to become kings…

No doubt!

*** Please see the 'Commentary' section.

Come Correct

Check yourself and come correct
because you have ample
means to provide positive examples.
Think about the lack of morals
you have "justified".
Violence and promiscuity
should never be glorified.
Instead of contributing to mind pollution,
you should be offering solutions.
Seemingly insignificant things that you say
are enough to lead a child astray.
There's nothing cool about
calling each other "nigga."
If it came from a White,
you'd want to fight
because you know we are something
much "bigga".
Nothing could be slacker.
You never hear White folk say,
"What's up, my cracker?"
Every female ain't a bit-- or a "hoe"
You want credibility, then act like you know.
Compared to illegal activity,
even shining shoes has much more dignity.
Children are very impressionable.
Peer pressure brings enough negativity
without it ever coming from our celebrities.
Talking about that weed and the forty ounce.
Consumed in obscenity and using profanity
so easy for a child to pronounce.
Talking about glocks and rocks
and living foul on the blocks.
Crime and violence in the 'hood—
No, it's not "all good."
These are all the wrong messages,

providing our youth with foul images.
How can we get rich by selling our problems
and making ourselves look like fools?
There's a big difference between addressing the negatives of reality
and making them look cool!
Why don't you admit it?
It's not about freedom of expression.
It's just about making cash!
If you were really "keepin' it real,"
then you would squash that trash.
Because trash belongs in a trash can
or some type of receptacle.
It should never be presented as socially acceptable.

Represent

Why do we blast
songs that forgot about our past
and sold out and bought into a
mainstream society
(the same that encourages the
white racist system
that has oppressed you and me),
tried to make us hate our Black selves,
and laughs while we kill our Black selves
and sell stereotypical images of our Black selves
and of our neighborhoods
and satisfy a money-driven industry
in the process
and forget that our identity and integrity
are much more important than popularity and wealth in excess?
Why do we idolize brothers and sisters
who brag about the money they have made
when they don't care about how bad they make us look
as long as they get paid?
We can't stand it when other people stereotype us,
but we don't even think about it when it is done by us?
You were made by GOD,
not by your environment.
You can walk with Him and rise above it,
so why die in it?
Most people in the ghetto are not living foul or selling weed.
We cannot allow ourselves
to be consumed by greed.
We are not niggers!
We are something much bigger!
Your true identity
is more valuable than riches.
Not all of our men run from responsibility,
and not all of our women are what they call
hoes and bit--es.

They claim they don't generalize
when they use these words,
but still no distinctions are made.
They glorify players, but don't think about
how they would feel
if their own mothers and sisters got played.
How can we see the exploitation of our sisters and not care?
Sure, they do it willingly.
But only because those jobs are
already out there.
Adult entertainment?
How you trying to play me, yo?
Adult entertainment
should not be played on the radio.
How can you play tracks that say
drugs are an acceptable escape?
Why is there so little substance in today's CDs and tapes?
Some of us use our bodies to sell our songs.
Since when did love songs
become tasteless sex songs?
Sure, it's all kinds of music—
not just a Black or a rap thing.
But the mentally enslaved
do not regain the status of kings.
It ain't about freedom of expression.
It's about making cash.
We need to recognize that some 'art'
is just trash.
Being Black does not mean being violent.
The following information has been kept silent:
The legacy of violence in this country grew out of a slave-owning,
Southern white "code of honor" that we adopted and named respect.
So, it's time to come correct.
The way we pretend to be ignorant might be even iller,
using curse words as fillers.
Since when did being Black mean cursin'.
However, we do mess up when we point a finger at only one person.

But how can we put the blame only on parents?
Are there any parents who can keep their eyes and ears on their children
24/7 anywhere?
And what about the parents who just don't care?
No adult can ignore our responsibility
toward our children--
Tell it.
No one can answer when you ask how much a soul is worth,
but some of us are still willing to sell it.
Rap on the whole is phat and all that,
but negative rap is wack
and we need to check that.
It is and should be a commentary on reality,
but the negatives in society should not be glamorized.
They must be attacked.
That's what 'keepin' it real' means.
Rhymes are not the cause of problems.
But why feed into them
with explicit sticker contents
when you could be using your skills
to help make a difference?
It's hard to get a record deal,
and so there ain't much incentive
to make a record with more positive than negative.
But there's a time and a place for everything
whether you rap or sing.
So, why not use your talents
to restore the balance?
Why not squash the images and messages of hopelessness
And return to flows for fun
and battles see who the dopest is?
Our 'get rich by selling our problems' entertainers
are just trying to get paid,
but they make small change
compared to the whites
who sit atop the industry.

So, why should we let some prejudiced whites use us to make themselves
richer and help maintain the negative image
of us in the media
while we get a smaller proportion
of the money?
Sure, in the industry,
we have some Black mo-guls,
but their main concern is making mo' money—
not making our image mo' better.
Thug and pimp want-to-be's
should never
be our role models
and trendsetters.
Music is not just entertainment—
no matter what we try to say.
Music is a way of life—
something most people cannot live without from day to day.

You better act like you know.
Before you sign a contract,
you need to take the oath:
I refuse to sell out just to get the papers.
I refuse to sell out and misrepresent
just to get the papers.
I refuse to sell out, and misrepresent,
and claim I represent just to get the papers.

Tyari Witherspoon

All Hail the Black Queens

There is something about a Black queen.
Her beauty beats all I've ever seen.
Strong sisters united will forever be.
There is nothing quite like our Black queens.
To lift them up, we must start.
Let us praise the queens of our minds and hearts.
They are queens in body and soul—
the young and the old.
They embody 'woman' and all that it means.
All hail the Black queens.

Black Is...

Black is bold.
Black is bright.
Black is beautiful.
Black was sold.
Black has plight.
Black is still beautiful!

Equality

Deserved, desired
Searching, reaching, finding
Order, justice, confusion, foolishness
Existing, hating, appalling
Unnecessary, despised
Prejudice

Black Oasis

Each oasis of accurate history
is far from the next, Black youth.
We must carry canteens of courage and determination.
To arrive at the truth,
we must travel in the heat of ignorance
through deserts of prejudice.

Pecan Tan

Caramel coated
with a rich chocolate center,
Black male is my gender.
My skin is light brown,
but I'm always down
with positive sisters and brothers
We all can keep it real.
Word to mother.
Brown is Black,
and Black is still Black
from midnight to off-white.
Not quite pecan tan
but still as Black
as the darkest Black man.

For Stevie

So influential.
This one is for Stevie.
Ain't many musicians whom I've so admired.
So full of soul.
This one is for Stevie.
His music always leaves me so inspired.

He is a man who cannot see
but still sees.
So, you see.
He's an artist in every sense of the word.
Songs full of consciousness
of this world we live in—
what's right and what's sin,
and what love really means
is what we have heard.

So influential.
This one is for Stevie.
Ain't many musicians whom I've so admired.
So full of soul.
This one is for Stevie.
His music always leaves me so inspired.

With brothers and sisters like him,
tell me, how can we
ever let Black self-esteem
just go under?
He's one of the greatest poets of all time
with longevity.
I thank GOD for Stevie,
creative Wonder.

Columbus Day

This goes out to Native Americans—American Indians
from the Indian in me.
I just cannot see
how they can give Christopher Columbus a holiday
when thanks to his so-called discovery
and navigational error,
an entire race of people almost got wiped away.
Even now, they have seen little recovery.
What are my chances of even seeing an Indian, today?
The myths of savagery are not enough to hide
or to justify the attempted genocide,
Thanks to greedy European expeditions,
came forced labor, harsh treatment,
the slaughter of hundreds at a time,
epidemic death from diseases
never exposed to before,
the robbery of their land,
forced departure from their lands—trails of tears,
being introduced to alcohol abuse,
being forced to choose
between reservation and assimilation.
Just like the enslaved African,
without their suffering,
would we even have a nation?
That still does not make it right in my eyes!
You better recognize!
Even if you cannot see how the human in me,
not just the Indian in me cries
in his spirit—swollen.
The west was not won.
It was stolen!

Racism

Any color nigger is ignorant
and knows no better.
This affects what he may do or say.
Stupid knows better, but does it anyway.
All humans are sisters and brothers.**
So how can the white racists claim to love GOD,
whom they have never seen
but hate their "brother"
whom they see everyday?
If they had been around
when Christ walked the earth
as human in part and divine in full,
would they have hated Him
for having feet of burnt brass
and hair like wool?
This is true according to the book of Revelation.
All people must recognize racism
as Satan's creation.

**Please see the 'Commentary' section.*

Glow

It is easier to grow
when we know
that it takes a little darkness
for us to look inside and realize
how brightly we can glow.

Ice Burns

They cast a heart of gold into the mud.
It's a pity that soon it will be their turn.
While the heart of gold is cleansed and shines,
those icy hearts of stone will burn.

Not the Way I Planned It

Treated like dirt, treated like doo-doo.
Treated like gum on the bottom of a new shoe.
Once confused, frustrated youth
Shut behind social isolation booth.
Visualizing facades of phony friends.
Wondering when cynical cycle ends.
Want to trust but distrust erupts!
Don't panic—
it ain't hot, violent, volcanic--
Just not the way I planned it.

Once fought fierce to fit in, but never gave in.
Now, just as back then--king of invisible men.
But no malice, no animosity.
But would appreciate some reciprocity.
But its time to take calculated risks again.
Time to drop the past in the trash bin.
Damage done, but healing comes—
Understand it.
Just not the way I planned it.

Flames

Sometimes my life is like flames
in the middle of the snow,
and it's pouring down rain.

Pain

What is pain?
Is it a day?
Does it remain?
Or does it go away?

Puddles

Puddles in the road that we travel.
Puddles in the wilderness
and puddles right near our homes
show that rain has come and gone.
Puddles we walk into accidentally,
and it seems it wasn't meant to be.
Why splash into a thing
unaware of the consequences it might bring?
Is it really worth it at all?
Should you try to leap over a puddle,
knowing that you might slip and fall?
Yes, even if it's easier to walk around.
You can never turn around.
Puddles 'round the way,
often temporary as the night
yet as plain as day.
A puddle is not to be run right through.
After all, the wise man watches his step,
and you should, too.

21

I've been here
for two decades and one more year.
People have always said that I was strange,
and still that has not changed.
Through my eyes,
I have seen so many days.
So many times turned away, turned away,
turned away.

I've been here
for two decades and one more year.
GOD has made me what I am,
and that ain't blue.
His joy inside my soul is true.
In my heart, I've survived all I've been through.
I have peace down inside,
but it seems I don't have you.

I've been here
for two decades and one more year.
Rejecting our corrupt society
can be lonely.
Wish that I could trust someone
outside of family.
Through my hands,
I won't let my chance slip away
even if today
seemed like just another day.

Walk On

Don't make the same mistakes
that you made then.
You just might fall harder
if you fall again.
It is time to put the past all behind you.
Just walk on when things happen to remind you.
The past is so old,
but tomorrow is so new.
So now,
what are you going to do?

Water Under the Bridge

Overlooking the past does not make it go away
or "make it all better" like a little child.
You must make up for your wrongs,
which cannot be accomplished
without being mature enough
to give a sincere apology,
which cannot be given without
first admitting that you were wrong.
Don't expect things to always go
your way or no way.
Saying, "well since you think"
or "well if you think I did you wrong, I'm sorry"
is just a cheap, easy way of saying,
"I'm too big to really apologize,
so you'd better take what you can get."
And whatever you do, avoid using the old cliché-
"water under the bridge"
when you have done nothing to make amends
because you cannot have water under a bridge
where there is no bridge,
and you cannot have a bridge
where there was no apology
because a bridge is a means of getting
from one side to another
while waves of water move along far away
when their beauty is not appreciated.

Wind or Wave

Free just like the wind
from any direction it is sent,
feel it blowing...around.
My thoughts are like the wave
crashing in my mind—
sometimes slowing me down.
But I'm not driven with the wind and tossed,
lacking stability.
Ears are ringing with good news
for I have the full use of all of my abilities.
Whether wind or wet, wild water wave,
I am free and not this world's slave.

Mr. Stress

Mr. Stress don't be playing no games.
When you've met him enough times,
you can call him by name.
At first, you may have seen his face
without recognizing his presence.
You may have shown strength in your eyes
and a smile on your face
even when pain was in essence.
Instead of running him off through the years,
have you refused to show weakness
and refused to show fear?
Have you been so busy being strong
that you repressed so much
when you should have been shedding tears?
Remember GOD
while you are trying to find release,
and soon, He will give you peace.

The End
(Tomorrow is Not Promised)

The Bible teaches me not to fear,
but it also says the signs are clear.
To be saved is what you really need to do.
Even if neither today nor tomorrow
is the end of the world,
that doesn't mean it won't be the end of you.

Different Cymbal

Sometimes I want to scream
at the top of my lungs!
Sometimes life is like going for a dunk
and getting hung,
or like getting dissed by a girl
who has you sprung,
or like having to smell the dung.
It seems that appreciation
should've come my direction
for choosing to be different,
but instead came rejection.
Although many things people do
are even more ignorant,
is it right to mistreat a fellow
just because he's different?
Being different was supposed to be good!
Yet, it often left me ignored and misunderstood.
Very few have even tried to understand.
Why not respect a fellow for having
pushed himself to be a man?
I thank GOD for my mother's prayers
and her teaching,
and for my being saved
after her preaching.
Been blind before, but not blinded by pride.
Although I know it's just my human side,
I get tired of making mistakes.
Never have I been nor will I ever be a fake
no matter how many times in the past
my heart did break.
I am a rope that has been tied too tight,
but the world wants to loosen the knot
because I believe in what is right.
Why do so many people still see not?
GOD has granted me wisdom

and little else much matters.
The meat of knowledge makes me fatter.
Inside my heart trembles.
It's really quite simple.
Pain deep inside clanging like a loud cymbal.
Yet, I am quiet and calm.
I remember the wisdom of Proverbs and Psalms.
I thank the Lord
for His Spirit and His word.
I cannot be stopped--will not be stopped.
Even if I get no props.
Even if I want to scream.
Even if this life is a bad dream.
Bad memories I blocked out throughout the years
made me fight back the tears.
But when the light is shown,
I will be proud to have known
that I was man enough to stand
even when I had to stand alone.
Silent and vocal words to GOD
I have prayed up.
Father, please forgive me.
My mind is still made up.

In All My Ways

Once again, I kneel to pray
for strength to make it through another day.
Remembering You in all my ways,
for life sometimes is an amazing maze.
Something inside won't let me cry.
Maybe, it's joy that won't let me lie.

Much is going through my mind.
What I've lost, please let me find,
and if they're not the things I need,
show me You have something better for me.
I feel that I've let myself down,
but in misery--don't let me drown.

Not to pray a selfish prayer
to my GOD above, who lives everywhere.
Sustain my loved ones--all my friends,
all Your saints, and all my kin.
Touch those suffering everywhere
for whatever the reason, thinking no one cares.

Thank You for the mind to pray.
Thank You for keeping me this day.
Thank You for all the blessings thereof.
Thank You for Your unending love.
These and all other things I pray and claim,
counting it all joy in Jesus' name.

My Guide

All my life and all my years,
Jesus Christ was always near.
He never let me fall.
Holy Ghost was always 'round--
Never ever let me down.
All I had to do was call.

When I leave this world, I am going home.
'Til then, I don't have to walk down here alone.
I've heard that heaven is such a beautiful place.
Once there, I will finally get to see His face.

Always looking up above,
I know I'm walking in His love.
My hand is in His hand.
Times of trouble come and go,
But somehow, He lets me know
He'll empower me to stand.

When I leave this world, I am going home
'Til then, I don't have to walk down here alone.
I've heard that heaven is such a beautiful place.
Once there, I will finally get to see His face.

Happy Birthday

Happy birthday, LORD.
The true meaning of Christmas
cannot be ignored.
In a wicked world, you were born.
GOD in the form of man
to feel what we feel.
People need to put away Santa Claus
and teach children what is real.
People will never know
your precise birth date,
but still we give thanks
for the day to commemorate.
I thank GOD for you, my loving, caring friend--
the one on whom I can always depend.
So, I'm really glad to spend
another moment to send
all my thanks and praise to thee
because you just keep on blessing me.
Perfect, precious son of GOD Almighty,
I've got to keep my hand in thine.
For I know that you take care of me and mine.
Dear LORD, my love for you is true.
So, I set aside this time for you.
You've never let me down or left me.
Prayers in your name are what have kept me.
There's so much to say,
and it all begins with Happy Birthday.

For You

For you, CHRIST died
that you might never have to sin and die—
but live life eternal
and never have to leave this world
and face hell's inferno.

Real Easter

Easter is not about new clothes, baskets, eggs,
and candy as sweet as honey.
It definitely is not about the Easter Bunny.
Christ is still healing in the world.
It's true, and one day
(not too late, I hope) you will see.
He hung on the cross and suffered and bled and died
for you and for me.
That old slick devil thought he had won,
but it only brought GOD's plan to completion.
Think of all He had to go through—
through out his miraculous life.
JESUS is Easter.
For our sins, He was born and He died.
He then arose the third day,
so that we might be saved.

More Than Any Other

Because of what I believed
and what I wouldn't do,
it was hard to make friends.
That's why it's so good to know
that JESUS is my true friend
unto the end.
Some things that people do just don't make sense,
and it seems so strange.
I never could understand
why people are so afraid of change.

But GOD...
will love you more than a father,
a sister or brother,
or even a mother,
much more than any lover,
and more than any other.

It seems the way we think
and the way we talk
are all so weird.
Why can't we understand
that change for the better
should not be feared.
That's the way it has always been,
and it has gone on for so long.
It seems that when you try to do right,
people do you so wrong.

But GOD...
will love you more than a father,
a sister or a brother,
or even a mother,
much more than any lover,
and more than any other.

<u>VOLUME THREE</u>

My Fire

Hey, girl. You are…
my fire.

You are…
my peach, my pear, my muscadine,
my candy card, my valentine,
my candlelight, my flame, my blaze,
my fire—
so in love and so amazed.

I'm falling deep in love with you,
falling like the morning dew,
falling like the autumn leaves
scattered by a gentle breeze.
Even through the rainy days,
when the leaves are washed away
I will love you baby,
always.

Hey, girl. You are…
my fire.

You are…
my harmonic melody
played in keys of ebony,
my violin, my clarinet,
my sweet and sexy silhouette,
my memories I cannot forget
my fire…
my fantasy since we first met.

I'm falling deep in love with you,
falling like the morning dew,
falling like the autumn leaves
scattered by a gentle breeze.

Even through the rainy days,
when the leaves are washed away
I will love you baby,
always.

My 1 + 9

Now, look here lady.
I'm gonna have to make you mine.
It's hard to believe that I have actually
spent some time
with someone like you—so sweet and so kind.
Your loveliness is on my mind.
How can I take my eyes off you
and your beautiful eyes?
I might try hard to look away,
but it's like I've been hypnotized.

I'm hoping you have more in common with me,
and I think about how wonderful it would be
if you and I were more than just friends.
'Cause I would make it better than a dream
and try to never let it end.
Can I just hold you in my arms for a little while?
I wish that I was the reason for your precious smile.

My everyday sunshine—
my only 1 + 9.
I wish that you were my pearl.
To me, you are priceless—
the sweetest and the nicest.
I wish that you were my girl.

And if you ask me how I can
tell you so much, so soon.
Well, if girls in the past have been stars, then
you must be the moon.

Body and Soul

Genuine—not artificial.
There is no one who is more special
or more beautiful
than you are.
Do you have any idea—
do you know who you are?
You should smile.
You should beam
when you see the looking glass.
You should always
know that you have…
self-respect and self-control.
Body and soul,
you shine like gold.
You are a queen,
even if
you have never been told.

On Hold

If you are not ready
to call it quits with me,
then tell me how it can be
that you're still afraid to commit to me.
What am I supposed to do?
I'm still so crazy about you.
You know it ain't cool.
Am I to keep on waiting for you?

Although what I feel is strong,
you know that before too long,
this will all get so tired and old.
I cannot put my life on hold.

By your side, I'd love to walk and stand.
But I'm not in the palm of your hand.
You should be my lady.
I should be your man.
So much time has passed,
and we have gotten nowhere fast.
When can we finally
put this game in the past?

Although what I feel is strong,
you know that before too long,
this will all get so tired and old.
I cannot put my life on hold.

Now, I don't really want to say goodbye.
But neither do I
want to wait so endlessly.
We'll never know if this can work unless we try.
You need to make up your mind.
I don't want to wander aimlessly.

Although what I feel is strong,
you know that before too long
this will all get so tired and old.
I cannot put my life on hold.

Although what I feel is true,
this will all soon get old.
I cannot continue
to put my life on hold.

It Cannot Be Denied

You let me down, and that you know.
Why not apologize?
I would do anything for you.
Why not swallow your pride?
If you still care, then take the time.
Our hearts have never lied.
If we are one, please recognize
what fits right by design.

It is not fair if you're prepared
to throw it all away
by playing games and thinking that
you can come back some day.
I know you're scared, and I don't care
if you know I'm afraid.
I will be strong enough to stand
and never run away.

I have forgiven, but it's up to you
to make things right.
I'm here today, but that does not mean
I'll be here tonight.
Although this wounded eagle
does not want to take his flight.
To soar away, still, I must say
that very soon, I might.

If I am yours, and you are mine,
it cannot be denied.
If it's so strong that you and I
know that we cannot hide.
Within your heart, just look and start
to let it be your guide.
If I am yours and you are mine,
it cannot be denied.

109

Within your heart,
just look and start
to let it be your guide.
If I am yours and you are mine,
it cannot be denied…
Should we really remain apart
because you never tried?

No Place I'd Rather Be

I remember when we were so close.
You were always around.
If everyone else turned their backs on me,
I knew you still would be down.
I never ever would said to you
that I needed some space
if I had known it could be the last time
that I would see your face.

Believing you still care,
you're always in my prayers,
and I cannot get you out of my mind.
Never would I want to
ever risk hurting you.
How could I have been so blind?

I write you letters, but it's gotten where
you don't write back anymore.
I've rung your bell about a thousand times,
but you don't come to the door.
I try to call you to apologize,
but you don't answer the phone.
I've realized that without you near,
I'm empty, sad, and alone.

I've been sitting here trying to figure out
what it would take to have you with me.
Because there isn't anything that I'd rather do
and no place I'd rather be...
than with you.

All Alone

Been deceived and I've been treated like an outcast,
but I don't see any use in calling names.
We might be real cool today, but on tomorrow,
"I'm not cool enough," and suddenly things change.
Some might know me a short while, then give undue pressure,
and it seems that all I find are playing games.
Or maybe, even worse.
They are with somebody else.
Or I'm too young
or I'm too old.
A heart so warm,
a world so cold.
So, I'm alone.
So all alone.
Much time has gone.
Still, all alone.

I have never claimed to be a thug or a player.
It seems that girls are gravitating to such guys.
Won't use you and won't run game 'cause I really care.
Can a real dog be compared to my wandering eyes?
Not when my girl is my queen,
if I had a girl, I mean.
Still, I'm alone.
So all alone.
Much time has gone.
Still, all alone.

How I have grown
and have outgrown.
I have reaped,
and I have sown.
But all I've known
is ending up alone.
So, I'm alone.
So all alone.
Much time has gone.
Still, all alone.

Fat Cats

It's racist, socioeconomic, political.
Still, we try hard not to be cynical.
The "little" man gets stepped on,
and it doesn't matter
to republicans as long as giants are getting taller.
But at what price?
The fat cats
are getting fatter
while the mice are getting smaller.
They must be eating more mice.

Mr. Hologram Man

Mr. Hologram Man,
dematerialize if you can.
You bought Uncle Sam.
You smile and cheese just like a real ham.
Master of illusion and lies.
Cost so many people their lives
through artificial terror in the skies.
Created a scare of terrorism
to improve your approval rate through false patriotism.
To you and your crew, average lives are expendable
if it increases what is spend able
by the top two percent
of the wealthy.
Man, you bent,
and it ain't healthy
for this nation and for this planet.
We now sit isolated from this world we inhabit.
Your attack on terrorism is a crock.
Before the world, you've made a great nation into a laughing stock.

If I may, I make this interjection.
You should be getting impeached instead of being up for re-election.
As if you were really elected the first time.
Better covered in 2004, but still the same crime.
False media claimed everything was under control
when once again, schemes turned my people away from the polls.
Minorities, including African Americans and non-English speakers
had their votes thrown away like some old holey sneakers.
People who never voted before
must now face a reality that's hardcore.

Gain our trust
after back-to back media suppressed, rigged elections?
Man, you must be high?
How many of our guys and gals gotta die,

and how many families gotta cry?
You still have not apprehended Osama, Mr. Hologram Man.
but your so-called war on terrorism almost destroyed Afghanistan,
including civilians,
innocent men, women, and children.
It was just a stepping stone for a war with Iraq...
When are you going to bring our soldiers back?
Your personal war has no clear objective.
Their blood pays for oil,
and their jobs mandate obedience to your directives.
Resting on a foundation of lies,
Mr. Nepotism blurs prerequisites with electives.

What is the Electoral College really for?
An outdated system still used by the rich to check the votes of the poor.
Still we do not abhor—
we love and adore
America or Babylon the whore.
Within an ultra-conservative cloak
for the Old South's racist mentalities rotten to the core.
I love the United States of America, but not its contradictions.
Perhaps the greatest place to live in the world, but not without restrictions.
In a land where I'se
been 'buked and I've been scorned—and still despised.
Even if it wasn't G-Dub, I realize
another shadow would still arise
'cause too many Americans believe anything they see on TV
and perpetuate a lost cause, gon' wit' d' wind fantasy.

Is anything really as it appears?
Your fake terrorist plan got my white friends living in fear,
unlike the real terrorism Blacks lived through
during slavery and in the nadir.
Our women raped—men and children—blood spilled.
In vain, to protect the purity of a race already mixed,
they destroyed Emmett Till.
Still we're not safe, even if it happens less frequently.

Many modernized lynchings have occurred just recently.
Still, I preach love not hate—peace not animosity.
Behold the only nation never held accountable for its atrocities.
Problems rooted in slavery…
A lasting legacy.
Racist cowardice vs. civil rights bravery.
Behind the scenes, somebody sneers
while my people shed tears
of disappointment and disgust.
Go ahead, savor your victory,
take a picture, and have an artist make your bust.
After all, its yours—you bought it.
Or did you steal it.
Mr. high and almighty,
I ain't tryin' to feel it.
Our nation has a wound.
You ain't tryin' to heal it.
It's better for you to exploit it
with false patriotism that creates blind zealots.

I'm so sick of these ignorant igneous and metamorphic rocks
thrown at us for resisting as you turn back the clock.
But our nation is the world's police?
A moral mask to cover the mark of the beast?
In run-down neighborhoods and schools we starve,
while you continue to feast
and protect your color/class-based privilege,
to say the least.
Back to the illusion—better yet, delusion.
GOD is not the author of confusion.
Documentation of your corruption is not limited to *Fahrenheit 9/11*.
You cannot ride pretext and subterfuge all the way to heaven.
GOD in the White House?
He's appointed you to set the world free?
No, GOD is waiting for you to do right by His people right here
living in poverty and social inequality
under this hypocrisy you call democracy!

As a point of reflection,
where was Colin Powell this election?
Well, here's the heads up.
They shut him up
'cause they knew that even he was fed up.
The only way to bring to an end to your ride
would have been in the unlikely event of a democratic landslide.
You wish you could run a third time
and really seal our fate
and make it possible later for the gubernator
to head our state.

If you got a lot of moolah and not a lot of melanin,
you can systematically trick those who refuse to see you as paper thin.
We hold these truths to be…suppressed.
Good ol' boys, apathetic whites, and sellouts are the only ones impressed,
while everyone else is distressed and depressed.
In the world's most powerful nation,
we have not coalesced.
The Patriot Act, a convenient way to cover your tracks,
subject us all to fascism, and the Arabs to attacks.
Do you want to be king or dictator—what's the deal?
Why can't you be a democratic leader who's for real?
One who protects each and every one of us as equals—
not just the richest white man and his land.
I'm not the only one who can see right through your hand,
Mr. Hologram Man.

Mansion in the Projects
(for Upward Bound)

You will excuse
me if I choose
to build my mansion in the projects.
I feel that it is a project worth undertaking,
painstaking, heartbreaking,
old wounds still aching.
No time for frontin' and faking.
Stepping on others
to get what you want is wrong.
Exploiting the weak
does not make you strong
I can't help the way I'm feeling.
So, I'm sweatin' it.
Self-destruction's where you're headed
if you can't help others and do the right thing
unless you know you're gonna get credit
and recognition.
GOD wants you to change your position,
lose your illusion
and confusion,
switch to fusion from fission,
and upgrade your ammunition.
Help somebody else get where you are
and beyond.
That's the only way
we shall overcome.
With access to resources,
the whole world will be ours.
Let us begin by giving our youth
sessions to empower.

If Darkest Heart Remains
(Enemies and Corrupt Leaders)

Much more than just words.
But after all I've heard,
it's getting on my nerves.
Please get off my case.
Don't slap me in the face--
slap out all the taste.

You treat me so unfair--
like I'm just a dog
with no bone anywhere
and lower than the dirt.
You don't care if I hurt.
Though, I would give you my last shirt.

Feigned good for applause.
Good for other cause
is no cause of yours.
Evil you devise.
Lies on top of lies.
The truth, you just despise.

All you have is pain.
No conscience and no shame.
All you give is pain,
duplicity, and blame.
If darkest heart remains,
the soul is lost in flames.

You seek to do me harm.
The opposite of warm
is what you have become.
For me, you lay in wait

and try to devastate.
But GOD allows me escape.

Your hatred grows from fear.
What goes on right here
is all vividly clear.
The enemy is havin' a ball!
You think it makes you tall,
what really makes you small.

You have so much gall
and refuse to hear GOD's call
and turn to Paul from Saul.
And that is not all.
So sad to know that pride
comes before a fall.

Where you gonna hide
when you're out of time,
Where you gonna run
when all is said and done,
and you find it ain't no fun
to get back all you have done?

For All the Critics
Who Falsely Accuse You
'Cause They Can't Stand or Understand What
They See In You

Do you judge the quality of a machine's work
by the amount of noise it makes or by the output?
When you don't know what you're talking about,
it's best to keep yo' mouth shut
instead of spreading your lies
and incorrect assumptions
or going around only telling half a story.
You won't be offended by what I'm saying
in the least bit
unless you belong in that category.
I often feel misunderstood
'cause I don't run my mouth as much as some people think I should.
Am I wrong for not being all up in
other people's business
or all up in people's faces all the time
being pretentious?
And as GOD is my witness,
I am a man, and I stand,
and I have always taken care of my bid'ness
one on one or in groups.
I've been one of the least obvious infiltrators
for GOD's troops.
I ponder and I wonder why
I "lack communication skills,"
and I'm "too shy."
But I can get up on a stage and "put it down"
and spit the illest verbs, adjectives, and nouns.
You will excuse
me if I choose
to use

121

sarcasm.
For sure--
'cause there ain't no cure
for these lyrical spasms.
It throbs and it throbs
'cause I'm so tired of being robbed
of what is rightfully mine.
Praise the Lord—I will be restored—
that's what "it is" time.
I'm about to get broke off!
So don't be surprised
when you hear it through it the grapevine.
I sometimes design secular rhymes—
sometimes design rhymes inspired by
the most Divine.
So when I flow for mine
and I go for my mine,
I rise—
it's time to shine.

Metamorphosis

Caterpillars, the other day
Too slow to run, jump, and play
Stop to rest for a little while.
Dream of turning to man from child.
But then, right before your eyes,
they become butterflies.

I Won't Let You Fall

My son, you have got nothing to fear.
Right now, I have got you here
for a purpose, a reason.
You will reap in due season.
I have called you to stand.
It's all worked out in My plan.
So, stand up and be a man
through and through.
Sometimes you feel all alone,
but you're never on your own.
And if you…
remain faithful to Me,
you will have victory.
And through it all,
I won't let you fall.

My son, your battle is already won,
though it seems you've only begun.
Act like it's already yours—
your victory, of course.
Just hold on to My hand.
The truth will forever stand.
There is no lie that can.
I will renew.
I never said you would see
a life that's always easy.
But if you…
remain faithful to Me,
you will have victory.
And through it all,
I won't let you fall.

Commentary

To my readers, first, I would like extend my heart-felt gratitude for your support. I hope that my words have been inspiring and maybe, even enlightening.

As we conduct our research and discussions, we must train ourselves to think critically and to 'deconstruct' the media. Even the best sources require us to 'sort things out' for ourselves. Here, I am not attempting to produce a thorough scholarly work. The purpose of a commentary is to make people think. I have selected a few topics for brief discussion.

Why *Stand*?

The purpose of <u>STAND</u> is to build up—not to tear down. This book challenges the reader to think about its content. While it is very much pro-Black, it offers something to everyone. I feel that "standing" or "standing up" is a universal theme that anyone should be able to relate to. It is significant because I have found that people too often stand for what is right only when it is convenient. For example, some people will not stand if it could make them unpopular or create controversy. Another example is the fact that some people fear what a person in a position of authority over them can do to them if they "stand up" or "speak up" more than they fear what GOD can do to them if they do not. We must respect authority, but there is nothing wrong with approaching a person in the right spirit. It is possible to tell anybody anything you want them to know without being rude or disrespectful. We should choose our battles wisely, allowing the Holy Spirit to guide us. We must also remember that GOD is the highest authority.

On Rap and Hip Hop

*** I have always loved rap and hip hop. I grew up listening to rap music, and in recent years, I have written much about the state of rap out of sincere concern. Although we must face great concerns such as 'de facto' segregation and discrimination in the education system and discrimination in the criminal justice system, also known as the prison industrial complex (Please see the next section of this Commentary, "On Racial Discrimination."), we cannot afford to ignore this issue of representation or to allow our former sense of social consciousness to be replaced by wholly commercialized values and instant gratification. Music is powerful. Because it plays such a great role in our lives, it cannot be dismissed as being 'just entertainment'. Consider the fact that rap's influence is far-reaching not only in the United States, but also globally. Hip hop has grown from an 'underground' culture in the mid 1970s to influence mainstream pop culture in recent years. Once upon a time, rap music encouraged kids to stay out of the 'street life' and it gave us positive images of ourselves while still acknowledging our problems. Yet, by the mid–1990s, much of hip hop music had mutated into an art form in which negativity became dominant, overshadowing artists having 'positive' or at least creative and socially conscious songs. Most of these artists cannot even get a break, today. I acknowledge that 'outside the studio' some efforts have been made to do positive things (such as hip hop summits and encouraging young people to vote), but that is not enough.

Artistry has suffered in the pursuit of material success at any cost. Unfortunately, standards have been lowered in radio and television as well. Positive efforts such as *Hip Hop for Respect* (2000) have been receiving virtually no airtime compared to songs that are filled with raunchy or stereotypical content. BET's "Uncut" (as a television program) and the problematic videos that appear on other music video shows are examples.

Bill Cosby's recent criticisms of the Black community remind us of the need to question the extent that negative images found in hip hop music reflect the Black community. Even though it does to some extent, this does not excuse artists or the industry from accountability. Although the problems in our communities might be obvious and destructive, they can be addressed in a more constructive manner that would avoid making generalizations and would be less likely to be interpreted as condemning people more than their circumstances. For example, consider the economic problems created by post-industrial America and the fact that political administrations in the 1980s failed to adequately address them. Some degree of negative representation can be expected, but it cannot be excused. The constant and consistent representation of black people as gangstas and hoochies is no different from this nation's traditional stereotyping of black people as coons, bucks, and jezebels. On a daily basis, black women are disrespected and black men are demonized. Images that ridicule black people and depict us as buffoonish, oversexed, greedy, underachievers will always be destructive, especially in the absence of images that are more positive, realistic, or balanced.[1]

We tend to defend blacks who stereotype themselves by claiming it is only entertainment or the result of capitalism. This is just as problematic as white racists persistently calling us niggers. Because centuries of institutionalized racism in America has tried to divide us and denigrate us, some of us allow ourselves to be manipulated and used in order to receive a small share of the profit. When oppressed people buy into their own oppression (even unintentionally), it is a product of 'racialism.' Racialism involves the continuing adaptation of racism to new times, and it includes racial insensitivity as well as both overt and covert forms of racism.[2] In defending blacks who stereotype themselves, we demonstrate that greed and instant gratification have become more important to some of us than intergrity and racial uplift. People who defend negative hip hop tend to argue that its criticisms are based on Christian morality and that critics conveniently take rap out of context. However, such an argument is weakened by the fact that the theme of a basic struggle between good and evil is a cultural universal. Also, the context of African American culture, experience, and expression does not excuse us from accountability. We are capable of maintaining cultural context without stereotyping ourselves or passing off commercialized negativity as African American culture.

Of course, negative images in hip hop music reflect an entertainment industry that largely ignores morality. I would even agree that it is erroneous to expect the entertainment industry to provide us with role models and that some of the negative images in today's hip hop music have always existed in American music. However, there was more 'balance' in earlier time periods. For example, even during the 'sexual revolution' of the 1960s and the drug use imagery of the 1970s, 'sex, drugs, and violence' music did not overshadow 'love' music. If people wanted raunchy entertainment, they usually had to purchase it. Unlike today, it was not readily available on the radio or on television. Also, compared to earlier generations, many of today's young people seem to be complacent regarding social issues. We must encourage young people to place GOD, community, and self-worth above 'bling,' 'thug,' and 'playa' values.

The media and American society as a whole bombard us with images of material success at any cost as well as poor representations of what it means to be a black man or a black woman. Still, the issue of self-accountability cannot be avoided. We must become more conscious of the images we portray of ourselves, and we must demand accountability from the music industry and its artists. As long as we support the sale of negative images, the industry has no incentive to change or to improve.

On Racial Discrimination

Two of the most serious problems African Americans face today are the de facto segregation in our school systems and the race-based criminal justice system, the prison industrial complex. Based on the neighborhoods they live in, too many of our children are forced to attend schools that are run-down and underfunded. They have limited resources and limited opportunities. An environment of low morale is often created, which continues the cycle of discouraging too many of our young people from pursuing secondary education or even completing high school. Discrimination occurs in the criminal justice system on every level of the system—from the police and the arrest to the court system and the sentencing. When these stories are told, whether through works of nonfiction or through works of fiction, they go unheard because they are not allowed to reach a wide audience. For example, the film *Prison Song* (2003) is a story told with conviction and a sense of urgency, illustrating poor schooling, the manner in which lives are destroyed by the criminal justice system, and how this combined problem poses a serious threat to the long-term ability of predominantly black communities to survive. Emphasis is placed on the fact that the system creates an environment in which even a young black male who has committed no crime could find himself caught up in the system just because black males have been demonized for so long in this country's history, stemming from the conditioning of white racist ideology. Since the slave period in this country, white people have been taught both directly and indirectly that blacks are savages who are naturally inclined from a young age to be backwards and to become criminals. The movie makes the strong case that African American males face odds that seem impossible to overcome once they become caught up in the system. Poor education and incarceration (and the link between them) are perpetuated by racial discrimination, and these problems continue to threaten the African American community. Please see the "Criminal Justice Statistics" section after the "Other Recommended Works" section at the end of this "Commentary."

*While the Equal Employment Opportunity Commission (EEOC), in general, has assisted many people, it is in dire need of reform in the South. It should be reformed—not taken away from us. Government agencies get away with discrimination just because they are 'the government.' Agencies such as the VA Regional Office Columbia, South Carolina only give the false appearance of equal opportunity. Such agencies hire minorities, but they fire most of them within the twelve-month probationary period. Unfair treatment for veterans and covert discrimination in hiring, advancement, and termination is the norm. They do not want too many of 'us colored folk'--no matter what our merit might be. I speak from experience. It happened to me in 1999. As a result, I was financially ruined, and I lost almost everything. I was forced to start my life all over again. A twenty-three year-old black male who had a college degree and went 'above and beyond' to assist veterans was perceived as eventually becoming a threat to the 'good old boy' way of doing things. They almost always get away with discrimination and wrongful termination. They are so well networked. It is very easy for them to lie and create false documentation to cover themselves. Also, the EEOC seems to have a conflict of interest. It seems that they share buildings and resources with other government agencies, especially the Department of Veterans Affairs. Unfortunately, cases drag on because of ridiculously backlogged claims and because the government is pleased to stretch things out as far as it can. It has unlimited resources while the vast majority of claimants obviously do not—thus ending most claims prematurely.

It is a shame that the United States, the world police, still allows racial discrimination to take place on its own soil. The right to vote, one of our most basic civil rights, is still challenged. In the 2000 presidential election, voting irregularities (especially in Florida) that indicated intentional discrimination were briefly mentioned by the media only to be downplayed and swept under the rug rather quickly. In 2004, irregularities occurred again. This time, the perpetrators were better prepared to cover themselves. The media was suppressed even more quickly and dismissed stories that contradicted the ridiculous notion that the presidential election was running smoothly. Discrimination based on race, class, and origin was allowed to take place again. Non-English speakers and elderly people were targeted as well. Anyone the Republicans perceived to be likely to vote Democratic could be a target during voter registration and at the polls. An unlikely landslide victory would have been the only way the Democrats could have overcome another rigged election. Unfortunately, more people than some of us care to believe are wiling to give full and unconditional support to a candidate or party who favors dishonest, clandestine measures that would begin to "turn back the clock" on the civil rights struggles of African Americans and other minorities and to further widen the socioeconomic gap in this nation.

On Race

**Scientifically, there is but one race—the human race. The traits found in all 'races' are found in the mitochondrial DNA of dark-skinned Africans (the world's first human inhabitants).[3] It is not unusual for dark-skinned people to produce light-skinned children, but it is "genetically impossible" for light-skinned people to produce dark-skinned children.[4] According to Acts 17:26, GOD "made of one blood all nations of men for to dwell on all the face of the earth..."[5] Not only does the history of Blacks (and gradually lighter skinned 'people of color') predate the history of Whites, Blacks dominated the entire biblical era, including the era of Noah's flood. The *Bible*, especially the Old Testament, is filled with references to ancient African kingdoms and their descendants. Black people dominated the world for approximately the first 2,000 years of recorded human history, beginning around 4,000 B.C. Much to the dismay of the White supremacist, the written history of Whites does not even begin until around 1,000 B.C.[6]

Please note that Noah and his early descendants were already Black. None of them, including Canaan, were cursed Black. Also note the fact that the ancestry of Jesus, the Messiah, (the line of Joseph) was both Hamitic and Semitic.[7] He came through the line of King David, whose lineage included Africans such as Rahab. Mary, the mother of Jesus, also shared African ancestry. Even though His spiritual identity is more important, I do not think it is right to avoid the issue of Jesus' skin color just because it makes some people uncomfortable. Why should we deny a part of our heritage?

Even though mixing with lighter skinned people would later become generally acceptable, archaeology, anthropology, and melanin testing demonstrate that each of the earliest civilizations—including Cush (Ethiopia, which at its height, included most of Africa, the Middle East, and part of Asia), Egypt (Kham or Kemet) and Mesopotamia—were founded by Blacks. Remarkably, the oldest human remains found in Europe even belong to black people. Black people and gradually, their lighter brown-skinned descendants spread across and civilized the entire world in ancient times. Even white eyewitnesses and historians such as Herodotus and Diodorus attest to this. Again, both the Bible and science demonstrate this.

White racism alone has kept the truth about the history of Black people from re-emerging and from being taught on a 'wide scale' because such knowledge destroys the ideology of White supremacy. The 'whitewash' of history only occurred so that some whites could justify the Trans-Atlantic slave trade, claiming that Africans were sub-humans who needed to be enslaved for their own good.[8] Today, White racism still exists in both subtle and not so subtle forms. On the other hand, there should be no effort to claim the superiority of Blacks or any other people of color. No 'race' is superior to any other. The human race can only be considered in terms of diversity—not inferiority or superiority.

Notes

1. *Ethnic Notions*. Writ., dir., and prod. by Marlon Riggs. Videocassette. California Newsreel San Francisco, 1987. This is an excellent source for the history of stereotypical black images in America.

2. Venise T. Berry, "Introduction: Racialism and the Media," *Mediated Messages and African-American Culture: Contemporary Issues*, Venise T. Berry and Carmen L. Manning-Miller, eds. (Thousand Oaks, CA: Sage Publications, 1996), pp. vii-xvii.

3. *The Real Eve*. DVD. 2002. Artisan.

4. William Dwight McKissick, Sr., *Beyond Roots: In Search of Blacks in the Bible*. (Woodbury, NJ: Renaissance Productions, Inc., 1990), p.16.

5. *Ibid.*, p. 17.

6. *Ibid.*, p. 31.

7. *Ibid.*, p. 16.

8. Joel A. Freeman and Don B. Griffin. *Return to Glory: The Powerful Stirring of the Black Race*. (Shippensburg, PA: Destiny Image, 2003). This book thoroughly explains the brief summary I give here.

Other Recommended Works

Anta Diop, Cheikh. The African Origin of Civilization: Myth or Reality (translated from French by Mercer Cook). 1974. Chicago: Lawrence Hill Books. (ISBN: 1-55652-072-7)

Bennett, Jr., Lerone. Before the Mayflower. Sixth Revised Edition. 1993. New York: Penguin Books. (ISBN: 0-14-017822-8)

Boyd, Herb. African History for Beginners. 1994. New York: Writers and Readers Publishing, Inc. (ISBN: 0-86316-144-8)

The Full Life Study Bible (King James Version). 1992. Grand Rapids, MI: Life Publishers International.

Karenga, Maulana. Introduction to Black Studies. Second Edition. 1993. Los Angeles, CA: The University of Sankore Press. (ISBN: 0-943412-16-1)

The Original African Heritage Study Bible (Authorized King James Version). 1993. Nashville, TN: James C. Winston Publishing Company. (ISBN: 0-529-10067-3)

This brief list is by no means exhaustive, but these books are great places to start. They also point to other sources. For your convenience, the ISBN is included where available.

Criminal Justice Statistics

"Black children are 46 times more likely than white children to be sentenced to juvenile prison."[1]

"Among children who have no previous prison record, Black youngsters are 6 times more likely to be sentenced to prison than White youngsters."[2]

Only fifteen percent of "the U.S. population under age 18" is black, but blacks make up forty percent of "the youths sent to adult courts and 58 percent of youngsters sent to adult prisons."[2]

Of the incarcerated population in this country, seventy five percent never graduated from high school.[3]

Twelve percent of black men between the ages of 20 to 25 "are incarcerated, according to the Justice Department." However, only 1.4 percent of white men in the same age group are incarcerated.[4]

Both black males and Hispanic males "are more likely to be imprisoned for minor offenses, while white men are more likely to be given probation for the same crimes."[4]

"Among youngsters imprisoned for violent crimes," a Black kid, on the average, serves 60 days longer than a White kid.[2]

"If the charge is the commission of a violent crime, a Black youngster is 9 times as likely to be sentenced to juvenile prison as a White youngster."[2]

"If an offense involves illegal drugs, a Black teenager is 48 times more likely as a White teenager to be sent to prison."[2]

Notes

1. *Prison Song*. Writ. and dir. by Darnell Martin. Co-writ. by Q-Tip. DVD. New Line Cinema New Yor and Philadelphia, 2003.

2. Rowan, Carl. "Too Many Black, Hispanic Kids Being Jailed." *Indianapolis Recorder* 26 May 2000, The Rowan Report: A8.

3. "New York State's Criminal Justice System: A Profile." *New York Amsterdam News* 2 Sept 1995: 10.

4. Tucker, Cynthia. "High Rate of Black Incarceration is a Major Challenge for Us All." *Los Angeles Sentinel* 30 April 2003: A6.

About the Author

Tyari Witherspoon is from Lancaster, South Carolina. He graduated from the University of South Carolina, where his major was Sociology and his minor was African American Studies. Presently, he is a graduate student at the University of Iowa. His goal is to earn an M.A. in African American Studies and a Ph.D. in History. He is both an artist and a writer, primarily of poetry. Tyari has been participating in Black history programs, open-mic events, and poetry readings since 1995. His first book, entitled <u>STAND</u>, is a volume of poems and songs that deal with topics such as love, spirituality, African American Studies, racism, and other social themes.

Contact Information

stand@tyari.com

www.tyari.com

www.ingramcontent.com/pod-product-compliance
Lightning Source LLC
Chambersburg PA
CBHW051410280526
45785CB00003B/1016